Kriss Akabusi on Track with the Bible

Illustrations by Mark Cripps

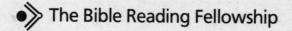

The Bible Reading Fellowship

Text copyright © Kriss Akabusi 1995

Illustrations copyright © Mark Cripps 1995

The author asserts the moral right to be
identified as the author of this work.

Published by
The Bible Reading Fellowship
Peter's Way, Sandy Lane West
Oxford OX4 5HG
ISBN 0 7459 3242 8
Albatross Books Pty Ltd
PO Box 320, Sutherland
NSW 2232, Australia
ISBN 0 7324 0930 6

First edition 1995
10 9 8 7 6 5 4 3 2 1 0

Acknowledgments
Unless otherwise stated, scripture is taken
from The Good News Bible published by
The Bible Societies/HarperCollins Publishers
Ltd, UK © American Bible Society 1966,
1971, 1976, 1992.

The Holy Bible, New International
Version (NIV) copyright © 1973,
1978, 1984 by International Bible
Society. Used by permission.

The Living Bible © Tyndale House
Publishers 1971.

Revised English Bible (REB) © 1989 by
permission of Oxford and Cambridge
University Presses.

A catalogue record for this book is
available from the British Library

Printed and bound in Great Britain
by Cox and Wyman Ltd, Reading

Contents

Foreword:

Off the track now

Kriss Akabusi is a man in a hurry. As a track and field athlete who won gold medals at Commonwealth, European and World Championships, as well as Olympic silver and bronze, he certainly was a man in a hurry. In his new life as a media personality he is always rushing from one appointment to another.

When Kriss Akabusi crossed the line in third place and a new British record time in the 400 metres hurdles in the 1992 Olympic Games, one phase of his life came to an end. That day effectively marked the end of Akabusi the athlete. A year or two earlier he had left the army, which had been his whole life since leaving school.

While sportspeople have often struggled to cope with the end of their career, Kriss Akabusi has taken each change in his stride. Just as he feels that the crucial switch from the 400 flat to the 400 metres hurdles in the 1986/7 season—which changed him from an average international athlete to one of real world class—was influenced by God, so he sees God's hand in the development of his life off track.

These days Kriss' infectious laugh can be heard on a variety of TV programmes. He is a presenter of 'Record Breakers', occasional host of 'The Big Breakfast', victim of Noel Edmonds' Gotcha Oscar, guest of Mrs Merton, presenter of 'Summer Sunday' or 'This is the Day' or 'Burst'. The list of his TV credits seems endless.

In December 1994 he had a new departure when he did panto for the first time, playing a specially created role in *Dick Whittington*. It was a great success with Kriss' exuberant personality establishing an instant rapport with the audience.

Kriss' ability to relate to people is one of his greatest assets. His appearance in a school can bring the place to a standstill. He is beseiged by requests for autographs—and that is from the staff. Whether speaking at school assemblies, giving motivational talks to business conferences, or representing the Duke of Edinburgh's Award Scheme or Cica Superschools, or debating in the Oxford or Cambridge Union, Kriss' message is the same. Work hard, achieve all you can, but ultimately without God you won't find meaning and satisfaction in life.

Stuart Weir
Director, Christians in Sport

Introduction:

Getting on track with the Bible

In *Kriss Akabusi on Track*, Ted Harrison tells Kriss' life story in detail. Sub-titled *The extraordinary story of a great athlete*, it finishes in 1991, and tells of Kriss' childhood, his army career, his marriage, his athletics and his Christian faith. It was in 1976 that Kriss got on track with athletics—almost by accident. He was sixteen years old and a signalman in the army:

Ian Mackenzie was the athletics officer and he noticed in the junior signalman a raw talent for running. Ian Mackenzie himself was a good athlete and the 400 metres was his distance. One day in the early spring of 1976 he was out running on the airfield when he was joined by Kriss. They ran for a while shoulder to shoulder, chatting, when Ian Mackenzie decided to get down to some serious training. As he accelerated off, he expected to leave the youngster behind, but Kriss ran ahead of him.

Somewhat surprised, the sergeant called out, 'Akabusi, what do you think you're doing? I'm supposed to be the fastest round here.'

A little later they had a more serious talk. 'Listen sunshine,' he told Kriss, 'you have got the potential to win the army championships.' And he even entertained the thought that the Olympics were within Kriss's grasp.

Ted Harrison, Kriss Akabusi on Track, Lion, 1991, page 54

AKABUSI!!

Through going into the army and through athletics Kriss became relatively wealthy. He had the money to get the home that he wanted and the car that he wanted. 'But those things didn't give me the happiness that I wanted,' he says, 'and they weren't satisfying me.'

Then in 1985 Monika and Kriss had twins, and they lost them. 'They were stillborn,' Kriss says, 'and their hearts were beating until Monika gave birth to them. That just got me thinking about life. What had happened to those two girls? Where were they? Their hearts had been beating—and then all of a sudden there were these two little caskets. What had happened to the spirit that was inside them?'

The following year, 1986, was the turning point of Kriss' life. He had gone to Edinburgh to take part in the Commonwealth Games. 'I went into my room,' he said, 'and there were all sorts of things in there, various little gifts and trinkets. And there was a Good News Bible with a blue cover. Just the New Testament—and for the first time in my life it was in plain English. I opened it up at the first page and I started to read it.

'There I was all of a sudden being confronted by those very same issues that I'd been thinking about. I was off and running! And before I knew it I was reading and I was hearing about Jesus. I'd heard about Jesus—baby Jesus and Mary and all that sort of stuff. But Jesus hadn't been really real to me. It was like a fairy story. Like Cinderella and Father Christmas and the tooth fairy—the stories that you're told as a youngster.

'But when I opened up that Bible I was confronted with Jesus. All of a sudden there was a context to this guy. And this guy said some powerful words: 'I am the way, the truth and the life,' and, 'I will give you life in all its fulness.'

'I was in a situation where I had everything. I'd got much more than I needed, but it wasn't giving me happiness.

'There was no meaning and no purpose to my life. I was rushing around and trying to be famous—and I was getting famous. I was trying to get rich—and I was getting rich. But I wasn't very happy with my life or with my relationships.

'As I went on reading, what kept hitting me all the time was what it said about sin. And I knew I was sinning in different parts of my life. But that wasn't what God wanted me to be doing. It just confirmed what I knew—because that wasn't what I wanted either.

'I had never realized that Jesus had walked on earth and that he had said so many amazing things. I had never realized that he had promised eternal life to anyone who believed in him. When I realized all these things about him I knew that I had a decision to make. I started investigating to find out if Jesus was a historical figure or a figment of the Bible writers' imagination. And I found out some amazing things. The Romans were rulers at the time and their historians mention Jesus and the effects he and his followers had on the Roman culture (Tacitus). The Jews, as one would expect, had ample documentation of the historicity of Jesus' sojourn on earth (Josephus). And probably more amazing than anything, what really blew my mind was the fact that the dating system we use was changed to demarcate the point when God broke into time and space to dwell among us. To this date my birthday, your anniversary, points back to the time when Jesus walked on earth—an amazing trick if he never existed. This got me really thinking about Jesus.

'I read all sorts of books, and I was really thinking about Jesus. Then I went to America and, on 14 April 1987, I went to bed feeling very frustrated and saying, "God, if you're really out there—Jesus, if you're really who you say you are—will you just let me know?"

'I went to bed and I had a vision—a vivid dream where I was on the bank of a river. I could hear a voice, and I jumped into the water and started swimming towards where the voice was coming from. It was hard work and the water was very turbulent, and all of a sudden the flow of the water turned me around and started taking me with it.

'I started to lose my confidence but I kept on going. Then all at once I was rushed up to this giant figure who was there in the middle of a great big fountain gushing out of the water. And I just knew it was Jesus. As I saw him, I heard him speak to me. He said these words: "Come to me those who are weary and heavy laden and I will give you rest. For my yoke is easy and my burden is light."

'As I heard those words I yelled out "Jesus!"—and I woke up. Then I sat on my bed and I just thought about Jesus—and I was so peaceful and so tranquil and so happy. I wrote all those things down and then I went to sleep again—and in the morning when I woke up I looked at my filofax and it was all there. Written down. My baptism by the Holy Spirit.

'That morning I went down to the track and I spoke to all the guys. All of a sudden all the factual knowledge that I had went from my head down to my heart. All my doubts went away and I was telling everybody about Jesus.

'I knew God loved me—and that he loved everybody else as well. That scripture just opened up the truth to me. All the questions that I'd been struggling with were starting to be answered—and the light was starting to shine in the darkness like the first gleam of dawn. That's how the book of Proverbs describes it—and I was reading that just this morning.'

The path of the righteous is like the first gleam of dawn, shining ever brighter till the full light of day. But the way of the wicked is like the deep darkness; they do not know what makes them stumble.

Proverbs 4:18–19 (NIV)

When Kriss read that Good News New Testament in Edinburgh it got him on track with the Bible—and the Bible got him on the right track with God.

'As an athlete,' he says, 'you go on track to reach a goal. And when you are training you are focusing on the one thing that you are training for—which is to run fast and to win the race. So you do everything possible to get yourself ready for that. You are on that track every day: training, preparing, concentrating.'

When St Paul knew that he hadn't much longer to live he wrote a letter to Timothy, his young colleague and assistant. He said that the Christian life was like a race—and that now he had finished the course and was looking forward to what lay ahead.

As for me, the hour has come for me to be sacrificed; the time is here for me to leave this life. I have done my best in the race, I have run the full distance, and I have kept the faith. And now there is waiting for me the victory prize of being put right with God, which the Lord, the righteous Judge, will give me on that Day—and not only to me, but to all those who wait with love for him to appear.

2 Timothy 4:6–8

Now Kriss Akabusi has got on the right track the Bible helps him to run the race and to stay on track. 'It shows us what God intends for us,' he says, 'and it shows us how to live. It talks about the good things that we do and it talks about the bad things. It makes us aware of our need for something more than ourself. It tells us about God, and it tells us about Jesus.'

Shelagh Brown
Commissioning Editor

Jesus the friend of sinners

One day when many tax collectors and other outcasts came to listen to Jesus, the Pharisees and the teachers of the Law started grumbling. 'This man welcomes outcasts and even eats with them!' So Jesus told them this parable:

'Suppose one of you has a hundred sheep and loses one of them—what do you do? You leave the other ninety-nine sheep in the pasture and go looking for the one that got lost until you find it. When you find it, you are so happy that you put it on your shoulders and carry it back home. Then you call your friends and neighbours together and say to them, "I am so happy I found my lost sheep. Let us celebrate!" In the same way, I tell you, there will be more joy in heaven over one sinner who repents than over ninety-nine respectable people who do not need to repent.

Luke 15:1–17

I am the light of the world

Jesus spoke to the Pharisees again. 'I am the light of the world,' he said. 'Whoever follows me will have the light of life and will never walk in darkness.'

John 8:12

1 On track with Jesus

For a lot of people in Western society, Jesus is just a swear word. Just a word they use. Just another word in their vocabulary. 'Jesus!' they say. 'Christ!' But it doesn't mean anything. It has absolutely no relevance to their life.

Getting on track with Jesus is understanding first and foremost that Jesus was a historical figure. That he actually was. And then understanding that what he had to say was something which involves you.

I was reading a passage today out of the Bible. Chapter 6 of Matthew starting at verse 25. In there Jesus says 'Don't worry!' And life is full of worry. Everyone's worrying—'What am I going to do tomorrow?' 'What about my next job—the next thing I want—my next this—my next that?'

But Jesus says, 'Don't worry! Seek first the kingdom of God and all these things will be added unto you. The sparrows are fed. The flowers have got clothes. And you will be fed. You will have clothes. All these things

Jesus the good shepherd

'I am the good shepherd. The good shepherd lays down his life for the sheep. The hired hand is not the shepherd who owns the sheep. So when he sees the wolf coming, he abandons the sheep and runs away. Then the wolf attacks the flock and scatters it. The man runs away because he is a hired hand and cares nothing for the sheep. 'I am the good shepherd; I know my sheep and my sheep know me—just as the Father knows me and I know the Father—and I lay down my life for the sheep.'

John 10:11–15 (NIV)

Being found by Jesus

'Suppose a woman who has ten silver coins loses one of them—what does she do? She lights a lamp, sweeps her house, and looks carefully everywhere until she finds it. When she finds it, she calls her friends and neighbours together, and says to them, ''I am so happy I found the coin I lost. Let us celebrate!'' In the same way, I tell you, the angels of God rejoice over one sinner who repents.'

Luke 15:8–10

you can have—but seek first the kingdom of God.'

Life is far more than things. It's far more than being the best businessman or being the best athlete. There's no problem about doing very well in business or doing very well in anything—so long as Jesus is number one. And that is the key to getting on track with Jesus. Putting him first.

To get on track with Jesus is also to understand about your life. That you are a sinner. We all are. But he wants us to come to him—and he doesn't want us to get cleaned up first. He says, 'Come to me as you are.' Then he will forgive all our sins and give us a new start in life.

> 'Come to me, all you who are weary and burdened, and I will give you rest.'
>
> *Matthew 11:28 (NIV)*

> Jesus said to the paralysed man, 'My son, your sins are forgiven.' Some teachers of the Law who were sitting there thought to themselves, 'How dare he talk like this? This is blasphemy! God is the only one who can forgive sins!'
>
> *Mark 2:5–7*

They were right. The problem was, they missed the point. Jesus can forgive sins, because Jesus is God himself—God incarnate, God become a man. And that is quite a hard concept to grasp. But when I started to read the Gospels I started to grasp it. I met the real Jesus and I started to understand who he really is.

He was born as a little baby. He really lived and he really died. He died on the cross—crucified. But he didn't stay dead. It says that he rose again from the dead and that people saw him.

When Thomas saw him he worshipped him. In Jewish culture it was blasphemous to worship anything else but God. Now Thomas was one of the twelve apostles—and he hadn't been there with the others on the first Easter Sunday. And he didn't believe what they said.

> One of the twelve disciples, Thomas (called the Twin), was not with them when Jesus came. So the

other disciples told him, 'We have seen the Lord!'

Thomas said to them, 'Unless I see the scars of the nails in his hands and put my finger on those scars and my hand in his side, I will not believe.'

A week later the disciples were together again indoors, and Thomas was with them. The doors were locked, but Jesus came and stood among them and said, 'Peace be with you.' Then he said to Thomas, 'Put your finger here, and look at my hands; then stretch out your hand and put it in my side. Stop your doubting, and believe!'

Thomas answered him, 'My Lord and my God!'

Jesus said to him, 'Do you believe because you see me? How happy are those who believe without seeing me!'

John 20:24–29

If we put Jesus in the right place then everything else (by way of finding the context) is sorted out. I don't worry about tomorrow. I've done very well in athletics. But I was very happy to say cheerio to my athletics because I was sure that God had my best interests at heart and that things would be all right. And they have been. I have gone on and I am doing other things. I'm on television, I'm in pantomime, and I do a lot of public speaking.

When I made my retirement announcement people thought I was crazy. But I didn't want athletics to be my god. It's so easy for your business to be your god—or your sport, anything you value can be your god. But getting on track with Jesus is understanding who he is, and what he's got to say about you and your life. And it's being in a relationship with him.

If you want to get on track with Jesus then the first thing to do is to be open. Say to Jesus, 'I don't know who you are and I don't know where you are. But if you're really there, and if you want to have a relationship with me, then let me know.' Just a simple prayer.

You can have great big eloquent prayers with great big words. But prayer is deep down inside you, and it's you yearning to meet God and struggling with God. It's saying to Jesus, 'Where are you? How come I don't know you? How come we don't meet each other?'

Be sure, if you do that, he will let you know. You might meet someone you've never met before and they will speak to you. God might open up the word of the Bible and speak to you through that, like he did to me.

I don't know how he will do it for you, but somehow or other God will speak to you. But he won't hit you with a sledgehammer. I had a kind of a vision in the end which made me realize that God was speaking to me—in a dream. For you it could be something subtle. But he will speak to you. He says he will. Just ask him.

'Ask, and you will receive; seek, and you will find; knock, and the door will be opened to you.'

Luke 11:9

Or it could happen the other way round. The book of Revelation talks about Jesus knocking on the door of your heart. He wants you to let him in, but he won't push the door down. You'll have to open it and ask him to come inside. If you do, then he will.

'Listen! I stand at the door and knock; if anyone hears my voice and opens the door, I will come in and eat with them, and they will eat with me.'

Revelation 3:20

2 *On track with sin*

In January of 1995 the whole of the media was full of the story of Eric Cantona. A top class international footballer—sent off the field for whatever it was he did. Then someone in the crowd called him a Frog and a lot of other things and Eric Cantona just went for him. It was real racial abuse, and he snapped. I'm not condoning it. But all of a sudden everyone was saying, 'Disgraceful! Disgusting! Yeah! Ban him for life!' Everyone was condemning him and making all sorts of self-righteous comments. Yet they themselves have never been put in Eric Cantona's position.

Jesus had a real good word for those people. He said, 'He who is without sin, let him cast the first stone.' He also said, 'Do not judge others, so that God will not judge you, for God will judge you in the same way as you judge others, and he will apply to you the same rules you apply to others' (Matthew 7:1–2).

The Bible says that each and every one of us has sin. And the funny thing is that our sin always looks worse

Sin and mercy

In the past you were spiritually dead because of your disobedience and sins. At that time you followed the world's evil way; you obeyed the ruler of the spiritual powers in space, the spirit who now controls the people who disobey God. Actually all of us were like them and lived according to our natural desires, doing whatever suited the wishes of our own bodies and minds. In our natural conditon we, like everyone else, were destined to suffer God's anger.

But God's mercy is so abundant, and his love for us is so great, that while we were spiritually dead in our disobedience he brought us to life with Christ. It is by God's grace that you have been saved. In our union with Christ Jesus he raised us up with him to rule with him in the heavenly world. He did this to demonstrate for all time to come the extraordinary greatness of his grace in the love he showed us in Christ Jesus. For it is by God's grace that you have been saved through faith. It is not the result of your own efforts, but God's gift, so that no one can boast about it. God has made us what we are, and in our union with Christ Jesus he has created us for a life of good deeds, which he has already prepared for us to do.

Ephesians 2:1–10

when somebody else is committing it. We could be put in a situation like Eric Cantona was—and then we'd be finding any number of explanations as to why what we'd done was all right.

Being on track with sin is understanding that each and every one of us is a sinner. We are not what God would have us to be. But nonetheless God still wants to have a relationship with us.

God doesn't deal with our sins all at once—although he forgives them all at once, the minute we ask him to. Then he starts working in us to make us what we can be.

Jesus didn't differentiate between sins. But we do.

The two great commandments

When the Pharisees heard that Jesus had silenced the Sadducees, they came together, and one of them, a teacher of the Law, tried to trap him with a question. 'Teacher,' he asked, 'which is the greatest commandment in the Law?'

Jesus answered, ' "Love the Lord your God with all your heart, with all your soul, and with all your mind." This is the greatest and the most important commandment. The second most important commandment is like it: "Love your neighbour as you love yourself." '

Matthew 22:34–39

'Do not judge others, so that God will not judge you, for God will judge you in the same way as you judge others, and he will apply to you the same rules you apply to others. Why, then, do you look at the speck in your brother's eye, and pay no attention to the log in your own eye? How dare you say to your brother, "Please, let me take that speck out of your eye," when you have a log in your own eye? You hypocrite! First take the log out of your own eye, and then you will be able to see clearly to take the speck out of your brother's eye.'

Matthew 7:1–5

As the Scriptures say: 'There is no one who is righteous, no one who is wise or who worships God. All have turned away from God; they have all gone wrong; no one does what is right, not even one . . . They have not known the path of peace, nor have they learnt reverence for God.'

Romans 3:10–12, 18

. . . God's way of putting people right with himself has been revealed. It has nothing to do with law, even though the Law of Moses and the prophets gave their witness to it. God puts people right through their faith in Jesus Christ. God does this to all who believe in Christ, because there is no difference at all: everyone has sinned and is far away from God's saving presence. But by the free gift of God's grace all are put right with him through Christ Jesus, who sets them free. God offered him, so that by his blood he should become the means by which people's sins are forgiven through their faith in him.

Romans 3:21–25

We all, like sheep, have gone astray, each of us has turned to his own way; and the Lord has laid on him the iniquity of us all.

Isaiah 53:6 (NIV)

In church we will accept people who gossip and who slander and who hate other people and who back-bite. We will happily sit there and listen to someone gossiping about somebody else. Yet we won't accept people who are adulterers and fornicators. We put sins at different levels.

But Jesus made no such distinction. There is a story in the Bible where the religious leaders of the day bring out a woman caught in adultery. But Jesus turns and says to them, 'He who is without sin among you, let him cast the first stone'—as if to put her misdemeanour on the same level as their petty indiscretions. There was no difference. It was all sin. The Bible says that: 'There is no difference, for all have sinned and fall short of the glory of God' (Romans 3:22–23, NIV).

Getting on track with sin is first and foremost to say, 'Yes, yes, I am a sinner.' And the Church is full of sinners—but they are forgiven sinners. So you admit that you are a sinner, and you say, 'Lord, I know I am far from what you would have me be.' Then God forgives you and he welcomes you.

On the day that you die you still won't have finished with all the baggage of sin that you have. But all of your sins will be forgiven and covered. And when you stand in front of him you will be clean. As clean as if you had never sinned. You will be as white as snow, as if you had never sinned before. Because of what God has done. Not because of what we've done. We can't work our way to heaven.

I went to dinner once with a woman who was a really wonderful person. She was always doing good things. She was kind to people and she was kind to animals. The sort of person we would all love to be. We were sitting next to each other and she was talking to me about my faith. She was a Christian too, and half way through dinner she said to me, 'Kriss, I want to ask you something.'

There had been a story in the media about a doctor who had committed an act of euthanasia, and this woman said to me, 'Kriss, do you think God can forgive the doctor who did that?' 'Yes,' I said, 'of course he can.' Then she said, 'I want to tell you something.' She started telling me a story—and as she was telling me she broke down in tears.

When she was younger she was a nurse, and she was doing geriatric nursing. One of her friends had always said to her, 'Look, if anything should ever happen to me—if I go comatose, or lose my faculties, you will let me die peacefully, won't you? You will administer something?'

One day that friend had a stroke and she came in to the hospital. The friend's eyes followed her all the time, and there were tears rolling down her face.

The woman who was talking to me said, 'One day I found myself going to the cabinet and getting out some pills. And I found myself giving those pills to my friend. But as she passed away I was banging on her and I was saying, ''No, no! Please don't go!'' ' She had realized what she had done. Then she told the doctor, who said to her, 'Don't worry. You have done the right thing. This happens on many occasions.'

Then this woman asked me her question. 'Can God forgive me?' I said to her, 'Yes. Of course God can forgive you.'

She was an old lady when I met her—and she had done that thing when she was really young. All her life she had been working away trying to get rid of her guilt. Being kind to people, being kind to animals, being kind to old people. She had been an angel.

I said to her, 'You can't work off that guilt. You just can't. But God can forgive you. God forgives each and every one of us. None of us are perfect. None of us can stand before God because we are perfect ourselves. All of us have to trust Jesus—and to understand that he takes our sin and forgives it.'

For it is by God's grace that you have been saved through faith. It is not the result of your own efforts, but God's gift, so that no one can boast about it.

Ephesians 2:8

I could hardly believe it—listening to that poor woman. Listening to her telling me all the things she was doing. And other people had been telling me all the things that she'd done. She was a beautiful woman, and she had a gentle spirit. But deep down she was hurting, because she was trying to work off this one thing that she had done.

King David back in the Old Testament sinned. He committed adultery with Bathsheba, who was married to Uriah, and then he had Uriah sent to the front line of a battlefield to make sure he got killed. So that was murder.

David had sinned—but he finally recognized his sin. Jesus says that whether we commit adultery or whether we think about adultery it's the same sin, and murdering someone and hating someone are the same sin. There aren't some small sins and some big sins. You're not a little pregnant or a lot pregnant. You're just pregnant!

David wasn't facing up to his sin to start with, so God sent someone to talk to him.

The Lord sent the prophet Nathan to David. Nathan went to him and said, 'There were two men who lived in the same town; one was rich and the other was poor. The rich man had many cattle and sheep, while the poor man had only one lamb, which he had bought. He took care of it, and it grew up in his home with his children. He would feed it with some of his own food, let it drink from his cup, and hold it in his lap. The lamb was like a daughter to him. One day a visitor arrived at the rich man's home. The rich man didn't want to kill one of his own animals to

prepare a meal for him; instead, he took the poor man's lamb and cooked a meal for his guest.'

David was very angry with the rich man and said, 'I swear by the living Lord that the man who did this ought to die! For having done such a cruel thing, he must pay back four times as much as he took.'

'You are that man,' Nathan said to David . . .

'I have sinned against the Lord,' David said.

Nathan replied, 'The Lord forgives you; you will not die.'

2 Samuel 12:1–7, 13

What that affair with Bathsheba showed David was that he was what God said he was. He was a sinner—and his sin was not against man primarily, but against God—and he needed to repent of his sin. The fact that he was the king didn't make any difference. Just because someone is the prime minister, or the queen, or the president, their robes and their office don't make any difference. Everyone needs to understand what God wants us to know—that every one of us is a sinner who needs the grace of God.

A lot of people don't become Christians because they say, 'I'm not a sinner! I don't do things wrong.' But that always depends on who they are comparing themselves with.

We might look at our neighbour and say, 'I don't do what he does'—and then say what the Pharisee said:

'Thank God I'm not like that guy there.'

But God says, 'You're looking at the wrong person. Compared with Jesus you fall very far short of the mark.'

Just that little blue stain on the corner of a hankie means the hankie is spoilt. It doesn't matter how white everything else is. If the hankie isn't pure white it's stained.

It was after David admitted his sin that he wrote Psalm 51. What he is saying in it is that deep down he is a sinner and that he needs to repent of his sin. Then God will forgive him—and David will tell other people all about what God can do for them.

A prayer for forgiveness

Be merciful to me, O God, because of your constant love. Because of your great mercy wipe away my sins! Wash away all my evil and make me clean from my sin!

I recognize my faults; I am always conscious of my sins. I have sinned against you—only against you—and done what you consider evil. So you are right in judging me; you are justified in condemning me. I have been evil from the day I was born; from the time of my conception, I have been sinful.

Sincerity and truth are what you require; fill my mind with your wisdom. Remove my sin, and I will be clean; wash me, and I will be whiter than snow. Let me hear the sounds of joy and gladness; and though you have crushed and broken me, I will be happy once again. Close your eyes to my sins and wipe out all my evil.

Create a pure heart in me, O God, and put a new and loyal spirit in me. Do not banish me from your presence; do not take your holy spirit away from me. Give me again the joy that comes from your salvation, and make me willing to obey you. Then I will teach sinners your commands, and they will turn back to you.

Spare my life, O God, and save me, and I will gladly proclaim your righteousness. Help me to speak, Lord, and I will praise you.

You do not want sacrifices, or I would offer them; you are not pleased with burnt offerings. My sacrifice is a humble spirit, O God; you will not reject a humble and repentant heart.

Psalm 51:1–17

God was reconciling the world to himself in Christ, not counting men's sins against them . . . God made him who had no sin to be sin for us, so that in him we might become the righteousness of God.

2 Corinthians 5:19, 21 (NIV)

3 *On track with forgiveness*

King David didn't get on track with forgiveness until he admitted he was a sinner, and that's where it starts. You have got sin on the one hand and forgiveness on the other, and you have got to go to Jesus to get it.

A lot of people go through life and are never really confronted with their sin, so they never really face up to it. The truth and the wisdom is that King David was a sinner—and that each and every one of us is a sinner.

Sin is contravening God's will for our lives—and we see people doing that day in and day out. We see sin in our news. We see people abusing other people. We see one country fighting against another country. We see sin when one man goes into another person's house and raids it. We see sin when one man looks at what someone else has got and wants to have it for himself. That is sin. That isn't loving.

Sin (in the context of absolute love) is putting yourself before God and others. Looked at in this way, it's not just what you do—it's what you don't do.

When we sin we aren't loving each other and we aren't loving God—and that's what Jesus said the two great commandments are about: 'Love the Lord your God with all your heart and with all your soul and with all your mind. This is the first and greatest commandment. And the second is like it: Love your neighbour as yourself' (Matthew 22:37–39, NIV).

For as long as you believe that you're all right, that you haven't committed any sin, that you're not as bad as the next guy, and that there are thousands of people who are far worse than you, then you'll never be able to have a relationship with God. You need to come to the conclusion that you aren't all you should be—but with God you can be.

That doesn't mean that you're going to be perfect—at least, not in this life. Even after David had written that Psalm about forgiveness he wasn't perfect—but he was forgiven.

We still sin once we're Christians—but we're in a new relationship with God. We're the children of God—the sons and daughters of God. God is our Father and Jesus is our brother—and our saviour.

The New Testament says that, 'if we say we have no sin, we deceive ourselves, and there is no truth in us. But if we confess our sins to God, he will keep his promise and do what is right: he will forgive us our sins and purify us from all our wrongdoing. If we say that we have not sinned, we make God out to be a liar, and his word is not in us' (1 John 1:8–10).

The Holy Spirit shows us when we're sinning—and we'll be getting on track with the Spirit in the chapter after next. If we know we're getting it wrong then we can start getting it right. Psalm 32 is another one of David's psalms about sin and forgiveness, and the first sentence sets the tone: 'Happy are those whose sins are forgiven. Whose wrongs are pardoned.'

And that is so true. Time and time again in my experience I've done something and I've thought, 'Gosh, Lord, I've messed up. I've messed up.'

When that happens you can go through a period when you think, 'I'm just not good enough to be with God.' But then somehow God touches you. Maybe you're at a church meeting, or reading the Bible. And you come to the realization that God died even for that sin. So you confess your sin and you get that marvellous feeling afterwards—and you know that God has wiped that sin out and that you're starting afresh.

You feel, 'I'm washed! I'm washed! God has made me clean!' It's an indescribable feeling of happiness deep down inside you. It's more than winning an Olympic medal! That God has actually forgiven you that sin that you can't forgive yourself for. He's wiped the slate clean and you're starting afresh. It's a new life, the Bible says, and that's absolutely true.

I can still remember that very first day when I became a Christian—when I read the Bible and God showed me that Jesus Christ came to forgive my sins. I

felt so excited that I could hardly believe what I was reading.

Could this really be true? Could I really start afresh? Could all those sins I'd done really be wiped out? And when you actually apprehend it—when you realize that they can—that's when you get that racing of the heart. You take it and you make it yours.

The feeling of elation is fantastic! Yes, it's true! And what I like in David's Psalm 32 is that he says, 'When I did not confess my sins, I was worn out from crying all day long.' That sounds strange—but it's absolutely true. When there's a sin preying on your mind, you try not to acknowledge it. But it seems to affect everything else that you do.

I often find myself in situations in which I know God doesn't want me to be as a Christian, and the Spirit suddenly reminds me: 'Kriss, this is not an environment that you want to be in. This is not a situation that God would have you in. This is not spiritually uplifting. This is not honouring God.' I could be in a situation where I am hearing people cursing and blaspheming, or making coarse jokes and flirting. And I am not trying to exclude myself—but you can sin by omission and commission, overtly and covertly. You don't have to wield the axe to be a murderer.

The Spirit would be telling me, 'No!'—but sometimes in the past I wouldn't always be listening. I'd be saying to myself, 'Push the barriers! Push the barriers!' And there were times when I'd know that I had pushed them too far. But I wouldn't acknowledge it.

And the strange thing was that then things started going wrong in my life. All of a sudden I couldn't communicate. I couldn't speak to people. I couldn't run races properly. I'd go out on the track and I wouldn't feel confident in my racing.

I didn't really want to go to church—and when I did go I wouldn't have the joy that I used to get there. I had conflicts in all the areas of my life. I had conflicts with my wife and I had conflicts with my family. Inside myself I knew that my mind, body and spirit were not one. They were out of kilter. Things were going wrong.

But then when I actually said to God, 'Lord, I'm so sorry. I've messed up. I know what I did was wrong,' then all of a sudden the world was a different place. When that happens then all of a sudden you're talking to God again. You can even say, 'Hello, mate! Hello!'

You feel a great sense of euphoria and you feel happy again. You can talk to God again—whereas before you couldn't. Before you might just read a bit out of the Bible, then you'd put it down—and you'd say, 'Father, forgive me for all my sins'—and then you'd turn the light out and go to sleep. But you wouldn't really mean it. Because you wouldn't want to talk to him about the sin.

I really understand what David was talking about: 'Happy are those whose sins are forgiven, whose wrongs are pardoned . . . When I did not confess my sins, I was worn out from crying all day long . . . Then I confessed my sins to you . . . and you forgave all my sins' (Psalm 32:1–5). He had to confess them—and then he was happy!

Happy are those whose sins are forgiven, whose wrongs are pardoned. Happy is the one whom

the Lord does not accuse of doing wrong and who is free from all deceit.

When I did not confess my sins, I was worn out from crying all day long. Day and night you punished me, Lord; my strength was completely drained, as moisture is dried up by the summer heat.

Then I confessed my sins to you; I did not conceal my wrongdoings. I decided to confess them to you, and you forgave all my sins.

So all your loyal people should pray to you in times of need; when a great flood of trouble comes rushing in, it will not reach them. You are my hiding place; you will save me from trouble. I sing aloud of your salvation, because you protect me.

The Lord says, 'I will teach you the way you should go; I will instruct you and advise you. Don't be stupid like a horse or a mule, which must be controlled with a bit and bridle to make it submit.'

The wicked will have to suffer, but those who trust in the Lord are protected by his constant love. You that are righteous, be glad and rejoice because of what the Lord has done. You that obey him, shout for joy!

Psalm 32

A guy in California, Hank Hanagraff, helped me to understand about sin and forgiveness. He said, 'Imagine that you are a judge, and you are a righteous judge. You know the law and you know what the law requires—that if you do A then B must follow. You have a reputation for being a righteous judge, and you never flinch from doing what the law requires. Everyone who is convicted has to pay the heaviest penalty, whatever the penalty is.

'Then one day a boy comes into the dock to appear before the judge—and it is his only son. He has been accused of committing a drink driving offence, and he is found guilty. The father looks at his son and says, "Son, I fine you the maximum fine. Five thousand pounds." "I can't pay it," the son says. Then the judge takes off his robes and comes down to stand by his son. He writes out the cheque for what the son couldn't pay.'

That's just a simple analogy of what God did for us. But, in fact, he did far, far more than that. He paid the highest price. He said, 'You have sinned, and for your sin you are required to pay the penalty of death. But I am going to pay that penalty for you. I will die that you may have life. Eternal life.'

The wages of sin is death, but the gift of God is eternal life in Jesus Christ our Lord.

Romans 6:23 (NIV)

Well then, shall we keep on sinning so that God can keep on showing us more and more kindness and forgiveness?

Of course not! Should we keep on sinning when we don't have to? For sin's power over us was broken when we became Christians and were baptized to become a part of Jesus Christ: through his death the power of your sinful nature was shattered. Your old sin-loving nature was buried with him by baptism when he died, and when God the Father, with glorious power, brought him back to life again, you were given his wonderful new life to enjoy . . .

Sin need never again be your master, for now you are no longer tied to the law where sin enslaves you, but you are free under God's favour and mercy.

Does this mean that now we can go ahead and sin and not worry about it? (For our salvation does not depend on keeping the law, but on receiving God's grace.) Of course not!

Don't you realize that you can choose your own master? You can choose sin (with death) or else obedience (with acquittal). The one to whom you offer yourself—he will take you and be your master and you will be his slave . . .

I speak this way, using the illustration of slaves and masters, because it is easy to understand: just as you used to be slaves to all kinds of sin, so now you must let yourselves be slaves to all that is right and holy.

In those days when you were slaves of sin you didn't bother much with goodness. And what was the result? Evidently not good, since you are ashamed now even to think about those things you used to do, for all of them end in eternal doom. But now you are free from the power of sin and are slaves of God, and his benefits to you include holiness and everlasting life. For the wages of sin is death, but the free gift of God is eternal life through Jesus Christ our Lord.

Romans 6:1–4, 14–16, 19–23 (Living Bible)

4 On track with God

Psalm 19 is one of the Psalms that I really like—because of the way it says that God speaks to us through all the wonderful things that he has made. They are like words—even though they aren't written down.

How clearly the sky reveals God's glory! How plainly it shows what he has done! Each day announces it to the following day; each night repeats it to the next. No speech or words are used, no sound is heard; yet their message goes out to all the world and is heard to the ends of the earth.

God made a home in the sky for the sun; it comes out in the morning like a happy bridegroom, like an athlete eager to run a race. It starts at one end of the sky and goes across to the other. Nothing can hide from its heat.

Psalm 19:1–6

What that Psalm says is really true in my experience.

Sometimes I have been on the top of a mountain. I have looked out and seen vast mountains all around me—and they have spoken to me about God.

I have looked up at the moon and the stars—and they have spoken to me about God.

I have seen the trees with snow on them—and they have spoken to me about God.

I've laid back in warm climates at night time and felt the warm evening air.

I've seen little bees busily working away.

All those things that are so wonderful have spoken to me about God—and I just can't believe that they all happened by chance.

If you were to walk across the desert and come across a Land Rover you wouldn't say 'Wow! This Land Rover just came out of nowhere.' You'd think, 'I wonder where it came from?' Then you might think, 'I wonder who made it?'

And if you were to get into that Land Rover, and look in the glove compartment, and find there was a manual in there, you'd say, 'Wow! The manual to this!'

The Bible is like that manual—and it's more than a manual. God says in it, 'This book tells you guys how you should live. If you read it you can find out—if you're humble. It tells you about Jesus and it tells you about me. I created the world through him—and if you don't believe in me you're a fool!'

'The fool says in his heart, "There is no God"'

OK! YOU WERE RIGHT!
IT WASN'T A
MIRAGE !!

(Psalm 14:1, NIV)—and St Paul wrote a letter to the Christians in Rome and said that ever since the creation of the world God's invisible qualities had been plain for everybody to see—in the things he has made. So no one had any excuse for not believing. But Paul had total confidence in the power of God to put people right with himself if they did start to believe.

What God did for me

All my life from zero to thirty I lived in an institution. And I am sure being a Christian was part and parcel of me being able to break out of the institutional life. It gave me the confidence.

If you're not a Christian, one of the heavy burdens you have on your shoulder is that this life is your life and you have got to direct it. What God told me is that man makes plans but God makes these plans fruitful and makes that fruitfulness last. If you don't believe in an outside being then you have to control it all yourself.

It's safe being in an institution, because people look after you. And in the army people look after you. There is a framework there, and a safety net. All you have to do is to live by a certain code. Then your money is going to be there every week. Your roof is going to be over your head. Your meals are going to be there. And your clothes are going to be there. You're secure.

You feel safe from all the insecurities that people have. And people are nearly always insecure, because they have very little faith in somebody outside. So they

The waiting father

'There was a man who had two sons. The younger one said to his father, "Father, give me my share of the estate." So he divided his property between them.

'Not long after that, the younger son got together all he had, set off for a distant country and there squandered his wealth in wild living. After he had spent everything, there was a severe famine in that whole country, and he began to be in need. So he went and hired himself out to a citizen of that country, who sent him to his fields to feed pigs. He longed to fill his stomach with the pods that the pigs were eating, but no-one gave him anything.

'When he came to his senses, he said, "How many of my father's hired men have food to spare, and here I am starving to death! I will set out and go back to my father and say to him: Father, I have sinned against heaven and against you. I am no longer worthy to be called your son; make me like one of your hired men." So he got up and went to his father.

'But while he was still a long way off, his father saw him and was filled with compassion for him; he ran to his son, threw his arms around him and kissed him.

'The son said to him, "Father, I have sinned against heaven and against you. I am no longer worthy to be called your son."

'But the father said to his servants, "Quick! Bring the best robe and put it on him. Put a ring on his finger and sandals on his feet. Bring the fattened calf and kill it. Let's have a feast and celebrate. For this son of mine was dead and is alive again; he was lost and is found." So they began to celebrate.

'Meanwhile the older son was in the field. When he came near the house, he heard music and dancing. So he called one of the servants and asked him what was going on. "Your brother has come," he replied, "and your father has killed the fattened calf because he has him back safe and sound."

'The older brother became angry and refused to go in. So his father went out and pleaded with him. But he answered his father, "Look! All these years I've been slaving for you and never disobeyed your orders. Yet you never gave me even a young goat so I could celebrate with my friends. But when this son of yours who has squandered your property with prostitutes comes home, you kill the fattened calf for him!"

' "My son," the father said, "you are always with me, and everything I have is yours. But we had to celebrate and be glad, because this brother of yours was dead and is alive again; he was lost and is found." '

Luke 15:11–32 (NIV)

organize everything in their life. But they still worry about it.

Now I feel that my life is in God's hands. I still work very hard. But I don't have to worry about what's going to happen in the end. I'm going to get there. What I have to do is to work very hard at what God's given me today. I've got to be a good steward of what God's given me today. I've got to work very hard at the tasks God's given me today. And I do work hard.

A lot of people are depending upon themselves to get on in the world. I think that's why so many of them do things that are against their own particular principles and ethics—because they have got to keep in with the group and they have got to keep in with what's the going thing. So whether they have to lie, beg, borrow or steal they'll do it. Because the pressure is on them. To keep their job. To keep the money. To keep up with the Joneses.

But Jesus said don't worry about it! God knows all about what you need. Just trust him. That's one of the things that he's saying in the Sermon on the Mount.

'No one can be a slave of two masters; he will hate one and love the other; he will be loyal to one and despise the other. You cannot serve both God and money.

'This is why I tell you not to be worried about the food and drink you need in order to stay alive, or about clothes for your body. After all,

isn't life worth more than food? And isn't the body worth more than clothes? Look at the birds: they do not sow seeds, gather a harvest and put it in barns; yet your Father in heaven takes care of them! Aren't you worth much more than birds? Can any of you live a bit longer by worrying about it?

'And why worry about clothes? Look how the wild flowers grow: they do not work or make clothes for themselves. But I tell you that not even King Solomon with all his wealth had clothes as beautiful as one of these flowers. It is God who clothes the wild grass—grass that is here today and gone tomorrow, burnt up in the oven. Won't he be all the more sure to clothe you? How little faith you have!

'So do not start worrying: "Where will my food come from? or my drink? or my clothes?" (These are the things the pagans are always concerned about.) Your Father in heaven knows that you need all these things. Instead, be concerned above everything else with the Kingdom of God and with what he requires of you, and he will provide you with all these other things.'

Matthew 6:24–33

What is God like?

Some people have a picture of God as a Father Christmas figure with silver hair and a long white beard, and some people have a picture of a finger coming out of the clouds like the hand of fate, but these are false pictures of God—really wrong ideas. But I don't have a picture of God. I don't have any idea what he looks like. But I do know what my relationship with God is like—and I know Jesus.

Because my father went back to Nigeria when I was just a baby I never knew him. So I think that is why I am more in tune with Jesus. I speak more with Jesus than I do with the Father, probably because I never had a father to talk to.

When I think about God the Father I think of someone who is less approachable. For me the Father is more remote than Jesus. I think to myself, 'Gosh, I could never enter the Father's presence.' I know that I can. But for me the only way that I can is with Jesus.

When I do speak to the Father I speak to him with confidence because of my relationship with Jesus. It's like Jesus is my mate and I'm his mate.

Jesus is every bit as much God as the Father is. But I can talk to Jesus whatever I'm feeling like. If I'm feeling spiritually great then maybe I'll talk to the Father. But there are other occasions when I know I've done something that I shouldn't have done and I'm spiritually down. But then I still feel able to approach Jesus.

I say, 'Lord Jesus, help me. I don't see how I am going to get to the Father.' For me the Father lives in unapproachable light, and no man can see his face. So my access to the Father is through Jesus.

For me there is a hierarchy in God, with God the Father at the top, and then God the Son and God the Holy Spirit. I know that is wrong, and that there isn't a hierarchy. They are all one. Three in one and one in three. But I feel comfortable that I have got the Spirit inside me and Jesus with me.

For me the Father is on a pedestal. People will tell me that I have got it wrong and that God is not like that. God is much more approachable. They say to me, 'God is everything your father couldn't be. He understands you intimately. Nothing goes beyond him. He knows all things. Nothing surprises him. And he loves you because he loves you, because he loves you, because he loves you!'

I know that the Father loves me. And I know that he loves every human being in the whole world. So much that he gave his one and only Son for us. That's what John's Gospel says:

> 'For God so loved the world that he gave his one and only Son, that whoever believes in him shall not perish but have eternal life. For God did not send his Son into the world to condemn the world, but to save the world through him.'

> *John 3:16–17 (NIV)*

God gave his one and only Son in time and eternity. I have got a thing about time—and in linear time Jesus died two thousand years ago. But what happened was for eternity—and it happened before time and out of time. Jesus is 'the Lamb of God, who takes away the sin of the world' (John 1:29, NIV), and 'the Lamb that was slain from the creation of the world' (Revelation 13:8).

In linear time Jesus hung on the cross two thousand years ago, and he cried out: ' "*Eloi, Eloi, lama sabachthani?*"—which means, "My God, my God, why have you forsaken me?" ' (Matthew 27:46, NIV). He was crying out to God for the first time: all the other times when we hear Jesus talking to God, he called him Father. But for the first time on the cross Jesus really knew what separation from God felt like.

Because of all that I am in awe of the Father. I feel, 'Take your shoes off, you are on holy ground.' Like Moses when he saw the burning bush. But Jesus is my mate. I can say, 'Hi, Jesus!'

I respect the Lord Jesus—and when I pray I use 'Lord Jesus' and 'Heavenly Father' interchangeably. But I will say to the Father, 'Holy God! Mighty God!' That's how I feel when I am in the presence of the Father—on holy ground. But Jesus is my buddy! He's my mate!

5 On track with prayer

One of the things you start to understand when you get on track with prayer is that you aren't going to get all the things you ask for—and further down the road you will understand why you didn't get them.

It's also about being really honest with God. It's being honest about everything—even when you're angry. Job was very honest to God, and he was also very angry. He said to God, 'Come on! Why? I've done all the things that I'm supposed to do—so why aren't you blessing me? Why are you doing all this to me? Why are all these things happening to me?'

At the end of chapter 7, Job gets furious. 'Are you harmed by my sin, you jailer?' he says to God. 'Why use me for your target practice? Am I so great a burden to you? Can't you ever forgive my sin?' (Job 7:20–21).

That's fighting talk—and those are strong words. Job is venting his frustration. His friends say to him, 'How dare you speak to God like that. God's not interested in that sort of stuff.'

[Jesus] said to [his disciples], 'Suppose one of you has a friend, and he goes to him at midnight and says, "Friend, lend me three loaves of bread, because a friend of mine on a journey has come to me, and I have nothing to set before him."

'Then the one inside answers, "Don't bother me. The door is already locked and my children are with me in bed. I can't get up and give you anything." I tell you, though he will not get up and give him the bread because he is his friend, yet because of the man's boldness he will get up and give him as much as he needs.

'So I say to you: Ask and it will be given to you; seek and you will find; knock and the door will be opened to you. For everyone who asks receives; he who seeks finds; and to him who knocks, the door will be opened.

'Which of you fathers, if your son asks for a fish, will give him a snake instead? Or if he asks for an egg, will give him a scorpion? If you then, though you are evil, know how to give good gifts to your children, how much more will your Father in heaven give the Holy Spirit to those who ask him!'

Luke 11:5–13 (NIV)

> *'Our Father in heaven, hallowed be your name, your kingdom come, your will be done on earth as it is in heaven. Give us this day our daily bread. Forgive us our debts, as we also have forgiven our debtors. And lead us not into temptation, but deliver us from the evil one.'*
>
> Matthew 6:9–13

But God is. It's just what he's interested in and it's just what he wants us to talk to him about. It's right to get it off our chest and to communicate with God.

If you see God as a distant God, who isn't interested in you but who has set down a lot of rules and regulations, then you won't pray like Job did. You'll say, 'Oh, Holy Father, may I speak to Thee now? Mine is just to do or die, mine is not to reason why.'

But deep down inside you you're really hating God. You're thinking, 'I daren't tell this to him. I daren't say what's really on my mind.' But that's what God wants. He wants you to say what's really on your mind. There is something cathartic about letting God know what you're feeling.

In the end God justified Job. God said to the people who had been telling Job he was wrong that they were wrong and Job was right. 'I'm angry with you and your two friends, because you have not spoken of me what is right, as my servant Job has' (42:7, NIV).

At one point Job had cried out for an advocate. Someone who knew what it was like to be human and who could understand what it was like to be Job.

I cannot defend myself, for you are no mere man as I am. If you were, then we could discuss it fairly, but there is no umpire between us, no middle man, no mediator to bring us together.'

Job 9:32–33 (Living Bible)

But now we do have an advocate and a mediator. We have Jesus.

Being on track with prayer is being up front with Jesus. Being honest with God. It's saying, 'Jesus, be by my side. Holy Spirit, be with me. Guide me in what I do. Father, lead me. Forgive me my sins. I know I'm a sinner.'

Being on track with prayer is also giving God an opportunity to speak to you. Sometimes we just say the Lord's Prayer very fast—Our Father . . . Amen— and we rush off. But God says, 'Whoa! Whoa! Come back! I want to say something to you.'

Then what God may say to us is, 'You are doing all these things, and really what I want you to do is to sit down and just be at my feet. Just sit down and relax.' It's like the Martha and Mary situation. Martha was doing all the right things. Getting a meal ready for Jesus. But Jesus said Mary had done the best thing— because she just sat down at his feet.

It's easy to go to God with a list of requests a mile long, and say, 'Lord, heal this guy. Lord, bring that person into my life. Lord help me to have more money. Lord let me have this thing—let me do that thing.' It's all right to ask for things—but we've got to have the right motive for asking.

What causes fights and quarrels among you? Don't they come from your desires that battle within you? You want something but don't get it. You kill and covet, but you cannot have what you want. You quarrel and fight. You do not have, because you do not ask God. When you ask, you do not receive, because you ask with wrong motives, that you may spend what you get on your pleasures.

James 4:1–3 (NIV)

I thank my God every time I remember you. In all my prayers for all of you, I always pray with joy because of your partnership in the gospel from the first day until now, being confident of this, that he who began a good work in you will carry it on to completion until the day of Christ Jesus.

It is right for me to feel this way about all of you, since I have you in my heart; for whether I am in chains or defending and confirming the gospel, all of you share in God's grace with me. God can testify how I long for all of you with the affection of Christ Jesus.

And this is my prayer: that your love may abound more and more in knowledge and depth of insight, so that you may be able to discern what is best and may be pure and blameless until the day of Christ, filled with the fruit of righteousness that comes through Jesus Christ—to the glory and praise of God.

Philippians 1:3–11 (NIV)

If any of you lacks wisdom, he should ask God, who gives generously to all without finding fault, and it will be given to him. But when he asks, he must believe and not doubt, because he who doubts is like a wave of the sea, blown and tossed by the wind. That man should not think he will receive anything from the Lord; he is a double-minded man, unstable in all he does.

James 1:5–8 (NIV)

Who is wise and understanding among you? Let him show it by his good life, by deeds done in the humility that comes from wisdom. But if you harbour bitter envy and selfish ambition in your hearts, do not boast about it or deny the truth. Such 'wisdom' does not come down from heaven but is earthly, unspiritual, of the devil. For where you have envy and selfish ambition, there you find disorder and every evil practice.

But the wisdom that comes from heaven is first of all pure; then peace-loving, considerate, submissive, full of mercy and good fruit, impartial and sincere. Peacemakers who sow in peace raise a harvest of righteousness.

What causes fights and quarrels among you? Don't they come from your desires that battle within you? You want something but don't get it. You kill and covet, but you cannot have what you want. You quarrel and fight. You do not have, because you do not ask God. When you ask, you do not receive, because you ask with wrong motives, that you may spend what you get on your pleasures.

James 3:13—4:3 (NIV)

When I became a Christian, my prayer in my athletics was always, 'Here we are Lord, back on the track again. Lord, help me to give you the glory—if I should win or if I should lose. Help me to be a great witness for you.'

Then if I lost I wouldn't kick my spikes over the track. I've seen guys do that. Kick their spikes over the time machine—or over the dustbins. Or walk off in a huff.

To go back to Eric Cantona. My prayer would have been, 'Lord, just help me in this moment so that I can keep my cool. I want to punch this guy's head! But help me Lord. Father, be with me right now.' It's just as simple as that.

I never really prayed to God that I'd win. Often when I was training I would think, 'Gosh, how much I'd love to win!' The European Championships, for example. And I would often say, 'Lord, I would love to win. Is it possible for me?'

Then as the season developed and I was becoming the clear favourite, I would say, 'Father, will I be able to do it on the day?' I think that's the best sort of prayer. I'd talk to God just like I'd talk to my wife: 'Monika, I've only got four weeks to go. Am I really going to do it?' I wasn't actually praying to win—but I was saying, 'I'd love to win, Lord. If I win it will be so fantastic!'

Then when I did win, all of a sudden it was just me and God. I went down on my knees in the middle of the track—and that was just between me and God. I was saying, 'I can't believe it's happening! Lord, this is just incredible—it really is happening, isn't it Lord.' God was right at the centre of my life—and I was up in the air.

I think that people pray instinctively, whether they are Christian or not Christian. I've spoken with men who came back from the Gulf War, and from the Falklands, and they told me that when you are down there in the muck and the bullets start flying then there are two things that grown men cry for. One is for their mother and the other is for their God.

Praying is a natural thing to do. We look to something outside of ourselves. We go back to the time when we were infants and our mother took care of us. You always go to your mum.

But when things are really tough and you know that even your mum can't take care of you then you go to God. Even the biggest atheist will start praying to someone. 'Help me out of this!' Sometimes he'll start to make promises. 'If you'll just get me out of this then I'll follow you.'

When you look death in the face, and you know that your Rolls Royce can't save you, that your platinum credit card can't buy you out, and that your relationship with the government of the day can't help you, then you go to God. And all of a sudden your spirit cries out. Prayer is natural to man.

Once you become a Christian and the Holy Spirit is in your spirit then you really start to pray and to talk to God. I don't think we need to be taught to pray. It's instinctive. But here are some pointers.

> *Is any one of you in trouble? He should pray. Is anyone happy? Let him sing songs of praise. Is any one of you sick? He should call the elders of the church to pray over him and anoint him with oil in the name of the Lord. And the prayer offered in faith will make the sick person well; the Lord will raise him up. If he has sinned, he will be forgiven. Therefore confess your sins to each other and pray for each other so that you may be healed. The prayer of a righteous man is powerful and effective.*
>
> *Elijah was a man just like us. He prayed earnestly that it would not rain, and it did not rain on the land for three and a half years. Again he prayed, and the heavens gave rain, and the earth produced its crops.*
>
> James 5:13–18 (NIV)

God is our Father—so we can say, 'Our Father'. We can say, 'Hey, Daddy! Lord, you really are interested in me! Dad, you have got my best interests at heart. Lord, before I talk to you, is there anything you want to say to me?'

The majority of my prayers are very simple prayers, where I'm just saying, 'God, I've messed up today. I'm really sorry. You spoke to me umpteen times about it. And lo and behold it's happened.'

Sometimes I say, 'Lord, I really am flummoxed. I really don't know what to do. Show me what to do. Give me wisdom.'

Or when I'm reading the Bible I'll say, 'Lord, I don't understand this. I believe—but help my unbelief.'

I try to get away from the idea of prayer being a set catechism—without any thought or feeling. Prayer is talking to God—and listening to God. But I've got to be very careful. Because sometimes I get to a point where I am so casual in my prayers that I never sit down and think, 'Now, this time I really am going to talk to God.' So then I'll say, 'Poppa, I want to meet with you tomorrow. I'll speak to you tomorrow at 4 o'clock.'

We do need to make these appointments and they are a very important part of the Christian life. But more often than not it's a more relaxed relationship—like it is with anyone you have a good relationship with.

Sometimes I've been walking up some mountains and looking at the beautiful views and I've said, 'Lord, you are awesome . . . .' There's a Psalm that I like—'O Lord, our Lord, how majestic is your name in all the earth! You have set your glory above the heavens . . . When I consider your heavens, the work of your fingers, the moon and the stars, which you have set in place, what is man that you are mindful of him, the son of man that you care for him?' (Psalm 8:1, 3–4, NIV).

'Lord, who am I? You're awesome!'

There are times when I'll say, 'Lord, I really want to serve you for the rest of my days. I'm so grateful to you, Lord. Help me not to get too haughty. How have you picked me out of all the men in the earth to be in my shoes? How have you picked me?' I'll think, 'Lord you are just too good!' I'll use the words of a song to tell him what I think about him:

Lord, You are more precious than silver,
Lord, You are more costly than gold,
Lord, You are more beautiful than diamonds,
and nothing I desire compares with You.

Lynn DeShazo © Thankyou Music

I can be more open with God than I can be with anyone else. I am reticent about opening up my heart to human beings, because the more you open your heart the more vulnerable you become. And human beings have got a way of playing on your vulnerabilities.

But I can tell God my innermost thoughts—and God knows them anyway. I will have been thinking some really vile things—but in the same breath I'll be thinking, 'God, I really, really love you!' I can't say that to a human being. I can't say, 'I hate you—but I really love you.'

There are times when I really open up and I really worship God. It can be because of something that I've seen, or because of something that's happened in my life. It can be just a moment of euphoria when I'm listening to other people. It can be because of something passionate that's happened to me, or something that's really touched my emotions. Or it can be reason. I can sit back and just think about the awesomeness of my body—and about the awesomeness of creation.

6 On track with the Spirit

Every one of us is a spiritual person. Every one of us is made up of body, mind and spirit—although we can't see the spirit part of us. And because we can't see it we sometimes think it isn't there.

But it is the Holy Spirit who communicates with our spirit and lets us know that we are not in tune. It is the Holy Spirit who enables us to continue seeking God. It is the Spirit who in the innermost sense and deep inside us communes with God.

A very religious man called Nicodemus once came to see Jesus. He came at night—probably because he didn't want other people to see him. Nicodemus was checking Jesus out—to find out who he really was. So he said to Jesus, 'Rabbi, we know that you are a teacher sent by God. No one could perform the miracles you are doing unless God were with him.'

But Jesus said to him, 'I am telling you the truth: no one can see the kingdom of God unless he is born again.'

Nicodemus didn't know what Jesus meant, so he questioned him. 'How can a grown man be born again? He certainly cannot enter his mother's womb and be born a second time!'

'I am telling you the truth,' replied Jesus. 'No one can enter the Kingdom of God unless he is born of water and the Spirit. A person is born physically of human parents, but he is born spiritually of the Spirit. Do not be surprised because I tell you that you must all be born again. The wind blows wherever it wishes; you hear the sound it makes, but you do not know where it comes from or where it is going. It is like that with everyone who is born of the Spirit.'

My spiritual birthday was on 14 April 1987, and I am sure that is when the Holy Spirit of God entered into me. All of a sudden my whole perspective changed and I saw everything through Christian glasses.

Every day now I think about God and about my relationship with God. And about what I'm doing and whether I am grieving God. I'm in a constant discourse with the Spirit.

Sometimes the Spirit will say to me, 'Kriss, doing that doesn't give the glory to God.' But I may continue to do what I'm doing. The Spirit says, 'Don't go on with what you're doing. It's not what God would have you do.' But I say, 'I'll be all right! I'll be all right!'

God's Spirit lets me know whether I'm right or whether I'm wrong. Sometimes my own sinful nature, my own will and my own emotions will override what the Spirit says. But the Spirit goes on grappling with me.

The Apostle Paul wrote a letter to the Christians in Galatia, and this is part of what he said to them.

What I say is this: let the Spirit direct your lives, and you will not satisfy the desires of the human nature. For what our human nature wants is opposed to what the Spirit wants, and what the Spirit wants is opposed to what our human nature wants. These two are enemies, and this means that you cannot do what you want to do. If the Spirit leads you, then you are not subject to the Law.

What human nature does is quite plain. It shows itself in immoral, filthy, and indecent actions; in worship of idols and witchcraft. People become enemies and they fight; they become jealous, angry, and ambitious. They separate into parties and groups; they are envious, get drunk, have orgies, and do other things like these. I warn you now as I have before: those who do these things will not possess the Kingdom of God.

But the Spirit produces love, joy, peace, patience, kindness, goodness, faithfulness, humility, and self-control. There is no law against such things as these. And those who belong to Christ Jesus have put to death their human nature with all its passions and desires. The Spirit has given us life; he must also control our lives.

Galatians 5:16–25

When you are on track with the Spirit you do more of what God would have than what you would have. And you are a lot happier! The Spirit comes into your life to make you realize how things really are. To show you that you're a sinner, and to show you Jesus. That's what Jesus said the Spirit would do.

'When he comes, he will convict the world of guilt in regard to sin and righteousness and judgment . . . when he, the Spirit of truth, comes,

he will guide you into all truth . . . He will bring
glory to me by taking from what is mine and
making it known to you.'

John 16:8, 13–14 (NIV)

The Spirit lives inside us, which enables us to live the
Christian life. Without the Spirit we can't do it. But with
the Spirit prompting us and leading us we can. We can
live a new life in the power of the Holy Spirit.

The Spirit helps us to communicate with God. It is the
Spirit who lets us know that our Father is talking to us
and that we are talking to our Father. And the Spirit lets
us know that we are the sons and the daughters of God.

To show that you are his sons and daughters,
God sent the Spirit of his Son into our hearts, the
Spirit who cries out, 'Father, my Father.'

Galatians 4:6

When you are born again the Spirit doesn't go away
and come back again. He stays. The Spirit is in you—
but you can grieve the Spirit and you can suppress the
truth.

But there is a difference between the Spirit being in
you and the Spirit being on you—being 'full of the Holy
Spirit'. When the Spirit is on someone then something
drastic is happening. That's what it says over and over
again in the New Testament. Peter is full of the Holy
Spirit, and then—'Boom!'

Peter began to speak: 'I now realize that it is true that God treats everyone on the same basis. Those who worship him and do what is right are acceptable to him, no matter what race they belongs to. You know the message he sent to the people of Israel, proclaiming the Good News of peace through Jesus Christ, who is Lord of all. You know of the great event that took place throughout the land of Israel, beginning in Galilee after John preached his message of baptism. You know about Jesus of Nazareth and how God poured out on him the Holy Spirit and power. He went everywhere, doing good and healing all who were under the power of the Devil, for God was with him. We are witnesses of everything that he did in the land of Israel and in Jerusalem. Then they put him to death by nailing him to a cross. But God raised him from death three days later and caused him to appear, not to everyone, but only to the witnesses that God had already chosen, that is, to us who ate and drank with him after he rose from death. And he commanded us to preach the gospel to the people and to testify that he is the one whom God has appointed judge of the living and the dead. All the prophets spoke about him, saying that all who believe in him will have their sins forgiven through the power of his name.'

While Peter was still speaking the Holy Spirit

came down on all those who were listening to his message. The Jewish believers who had come from Joppa with Peter were amazed that God had poured out his gift of the Holy Spirit on the Gentiles also. For they heard them speaking in strange tongues and praising God's greatness. Peter spoke up: 'These people have received the Holy Spirit, just as we also did. Can anyone, then, stop them from being baptized with water?' So he ordered them to be baptized in the name of Jesus Christ.

Acts 10:34–48

The Spirit is always on track with us, but we aren't always on track with the Spirit. There's a difference between the Spirit being with us, and our being aware of it, and the Spirit being there when we aren't taking any notice.

The Spirit is the one who helps us to pray. Sometimes we just don't know what to pray, and we're desperate. We're groaning inside—maybe because we've messed something up, or because someone we know is in some sort of mess.

The Holy Spirit helps us with our daily problems and in our praying. For we don't even know what we should pray for, nor how to pray as we should; but the Holy Spirit prays for us with such feeling that it cannot be expressed in words. And the Father who knows all hearts knows, of

course, what the Spirit is saying as he pleads for us in harmony with God's own will.

Romans 8:26–27 (Living Bible)

The Holy Spirit is the Spirit of Jesus—so if we are born again and we are Christians then we have Jesus living in us. When he was telling his disciples that he was going to leave them, he told them that it would be better for them that he went away. They couldn't understand. But in the future he would be living inside them—so he would be with them all the time. The Holy Spirit is God with us, or within us.

'I am telling you the truth: it is better for you that I go away, because if I do not go, the Helper will not come to you. But if I do go away, I will send him to you.'

John 16:7

'Whoever loves me will obey my teaching. My Father will love him, and my Father and I will come to him and live with him. Whoever does not love me does not obey my teaching. And the teaching you have heard is not mine, but comes from the Father, who sent me.

'I have told you this while I am still with you. The Helper, the Holy Spirit, whom the Father will send in my name, will teach you everything and make you remember all that I have told you.'

John 14:23–26 (GNB)

If the Spirit of God, who raised up Jesus from the dead, lives in you, he will make your dying bodies live again after you die, by means of this same Holy Spirit living within you.

So, dear brothers, you have no obligations whatever to your old sinful nature to do what it begs you do. For if you keep on following it you are lost and will perish, but if through the power of the Holy Spirit you crush it and its evil deeds, you shall live. For all who are led by the Spirit of God are sons of God.

And so we should not be like cringing, fearful slaves, but we should behave like God's very own children, adopted into the bosom of his family, and calling to him, 'Father, Father.' For his Holy Spirit speaks to us deep in our hearts, and tells us that we really are God's children. And since we are his children, we will share his treasures—for all God gives to his Son Jesus is now ours too. But if we are to share his glory, we must also share his suffering.

Yet what we suffer now is nothing compared to the glory he will give us later. For all creation is waiting patiently and hopefully for that future day when God will resurrect his children. On that day thorns and thistles, sin, death and decay—the things that overcame the world against its will at God's command—will all disappear, and the world around us will share in the glorious freedom from sin which God's children enjoy.

For we know that even the things of nature, like animals and plants, suffer in sickness and death, but these are 'labour pains' as they await this great event. And even we Christians, although we have the Holy Spirit within us as a foretaste of future glory, also groan to be released from pain and suffering. We, too, wait anxiously for that day when God will give us our full rights as his children, including the new bodies he has promised us—bodies that will never be sick again and will never die.

We are saved by trusting. And trusting means looking forward to getting something we don't yet have—for a man who already has something doesn't need to hope and trust that he will get it. But if we must keep trusting God for something that hasn't happened yet, it teaches us to wait patiently and confidently.

And in the same way—by our faith—the Holy Spirit helps us with our daily problems and in our praying. For we don't even know what we should pray for, nor how to pray as we should, but the Holy Spirit prays for us with such feeling that it cannot be expressed in words. And the Father who knows all hearts knows, of course, what the Spirit is saying as he pleads for us in harmony with God's own will. And we know that all that happens to us is working for our good if we love God and are fitting in with his plans.

Romans 8:11–28 (Living Bible)

7 *On track with life*

If there was no God I would be an Epicurean. I would 'eat, drink and be merry, for tomorrow I die'. That would be me.

There are many people like that. People who think that life is about enjoying themselves. About making a name for themselves. About making a lot of money so that they can do all the things that they want to do.

I lived my life like that for twenty-seven years. Believing that what I could see and touch and enjoy was all there was to life. But then I started asking questions. What is life all about? Is there a purpose to life? Or is this all that there is of it? We snuff it and then it's all over. I started asking those questions when our two little girls died—when they were stillborn.

What is the meaning of life? Some people once came to my door and asked me some basic questions. 'Have you ever thought what life is all about? Have you ever thought about the beginning of the world? Did it just happen by blind chance—or was there a design to it?'

They asked me the questions that I had been asking myself. I had been looking up at the sky and the stars and wondering. Did they just happen? Or was there a design to it? I'd been thinking about the wonder and the miracle of life. If it all happened by chance then how did we manage to continue? I was thinking about the miracle of breathing in my lungs—and this little heart of mine continuing to pump every second of every day. Why didn't it just stop?

It was those sorts of questions that I was asking. And I was looking for a purpose and a meaning to life.

There is far more to life than the physical three-dimensional world. There is physical life and there is eternal life, and when we have that dimension to life we are in a relationship with God—and his Spirit is in a relationship with our Spirit. And even though we die physically we don't die spiritually. John 3:16 is the big verse about that: 'For God so loved the world that he gave his one and only Son, that whoever believes in him shall not perish but have eternal life.'

That verse tells us two things. God has done something. But he requires us to do something. God prepared the way. God so loved each and every single one of us that he died for us. But that in itself doesn't give us eternal life. What God has done is effective only for those who will accept what he has done.

God won't force you to be with him. God has done his bit. He says, 'I have prepared the way. It is for each and every one of you.' But you have got to believe.

If you do believe he will give you eternal life. And he will give you a fulfilled life. That's not to say that in between you won't go astray. It's not to say that in between you won't feel that God doesn't love you. But God did A so that B will happen: he gave his Son *so that* whoever believes in him will have eternal life. I am putting that very simply. And the key word is 'believes': 'whosoever believes in him shall not perish but have eternal life . . .'

That belief is a belief in which you entrust yourself to Jesus. It's not just acquiescence—not just saying, 'Oh, I believe.'

It's the belief of the man who saw the tightrope walker wheeling a barrow across Niagara Falls—and the tightrope walker says to him, 'I can take you across, too, if you'll get in.' So he does get in, because he believes what he says. It's not the person who stands on the edge and says, 'Yeah, I believe you can do it.' It's about jumping into the wheelbarrow.

When Jesus was talking to Nicodemus about being born again Nicodemus was saying, 'I'm a grown man. Are you telling me I've got to go back in the womb again?' And Jesus says, 'No, don't be silly.' So he is obviously not talking about physical rebirth. Jesus is saying to Nicodemus that he needs a rebirth of his mind and his spirit.

As human beings we have a body, a spirit and a soul, and our soul rules our body. What I think God wants is our spirit to rule our soul and our body so that the spirit comes on top. But that only happens when we are born of the Spirit.

'Flesh gives birth to flesh, but the Spirit gives birth to spirit. You should not be surprised at my saying, "You must be born again." The wind blows wherever it pleases. You hear its sound, but you cannot tell where it comes from or where it is going. So it is with everyone born of the Spirit.'

John 3:6–8 (NIV)

It's a process, this journey. You grow and you grow—and you start off like a little baby. Babies get hungry, and they have to be fed—and if they aren't fed they start crying. 'Be like newborn babies,' wrote the Apostle Peter, 'always thirsty for the pure spiritual milk, so that by drinking it you may grow up and be saved' (1 Peter 2:2). And the spiritual milk that feeds the new little spiritual baby is the word of God, the scriptures.

When was I born again as a Christian? Was I a Christian the day I read the Bible and I met God? Or was I a Christian when God grabbed hold of me in a real way and shook me. Was I born a Christian? Does my acceptance of Christ just prove that I was a Christian? Did I become a Christian that day? It says in the Bible that our names were written in 'the Lamb's book of life' before the foundation of the world. So maybe what happened to me in 1987 just confirmed what God already knew. There are several ways of looking at it—but I know that I've got a relationship with God now. With Jesus. And it's great.

*I have been talking to you as though you were still
just babies in the Christian life, who are not
following the Lord, but your own desires: I
cannot talk to you as I would to healthy Christians,
who are filled with the Spirit. I have had to feed
you with milk and not with solid food, because
you couldn't digest anything stronger. And even
now you still have to be fed on milk. For you are
still only baby Christians, controlled by your own
desires, not God's.*

1 Corinthians 3:1–3 (Living Bible)

*There is much we have to say . . . but it is hard to
explain to you, because you are so slow to
understand. There has been enough time for you
to be teachers—yet you still need someone to
teach you the first lessons of God's message.*

*Instead of eating solid food, you still have to
drink milk. Anyone who has to drink milk is still a
child, without any experience in the matter of
right and wrong. Solid food, on the other hand, is
for adults, who through practice are able to
distinguish between good and evil.*

*Let us go forward, then, to mature teaching and
leave behind us the first lessons of the Christian
message . . . Let us go forward!*

Hebrews 5:11—6:3

8 On track with death

First and foremost to me death is a reality. Each and every one of us is dying day by day—slowly, slowly dying. And to get on track with death is to acknowledge that fact.

There is a simple syllogism. All humans die. I am human. I am going to die. Say that to the youth and they might laugh in your face. Say it to an older person and they may show more discernment. So far the odds are 1:1 that we are all going to make it—we are all going to die. No one is going to escape.

Death is the final experience. Death is something that none of us who is living has ever experienced—but one day we are going to experience it.

When Monika's grandma died I was going through the Bible and I read Ecclesiastes chapter 7. It says there that wisdom is found in the house of mourning—and Ecclesiastes 7:24 is so important to me that I've got it on my private number plate: ECC 724. It means two very important things to me.

What is wisdom?

The first one is this: Wisdom—what is it? 'Whatever wisdom may be, it is far off and most profound—who can discover it?' (Ecclesiastes 7:24, NIV). It's a most profound question.

What is it all about? Where are we going? Where did we come from? Is there a God? All those questions are matters of wisdom—and if we ask where we can find wisdom the answer the Bible gives is this: 'The fear of the Lord is the beginning of wisdom' (Proverbs 9:10, NIV).

What that means to me is that wisdom is knowing why you do what you do, and what the motivating factor is for what you do. It's considering the end of all things before you begin.

If you have a philosophy that 'this is it and this is all of it, and what we are experiencing now is what it is', then your particular sort of wisdom (conventional wisdom) is: 'Grab what you can and do what you can while you can.' The end justifies the means, and in that sort of scenario it's not crime that's wrong. It's getting caught.

But what the Bible has taught me is that the fear of the Lord is the beginning of wisdom. That's not to say that I shake every time I think about God. But it's the knowledge that God is watching us. God is watching you and watching me. God has got a plan for my life and a plan for your life—and there is a reason for living.

There is more to life than meets the eye. It isn't just that I was born and I will die and after death there is nothing. There is something else. And for me the realization that all I see and touch and feel in this world is just a small part of eternity has changed the whole direction of my life.

Where can I find wisdom?

The second important thing that ECC 724 means to me is in Ecclesiastes 7:2 and 7:4, because they say that wisdom is found in the house of mourning.

> **It is better to go to a house of mourning than to go to a house of feasting, for death is the destiny of every man; the living should take this to heart.**

Ecclesiastes 7:2

> **The heart of the wise is in the house of mourning but the heart of fools is in the house of pleasure.**

Ecclesiastes 7:4

Wisdom is found in the house of mourning. Wisdom is found in death. The fact is that when you look towards the end, to death, you begin to understand.

Death does not have to be feared if you believe that death is the door to eternal life. That when you die you move from the shadow of things to the reality of things. The Bible says that on this side of death, on this side of that door, we see dimly. We see only a shadow of things. But when we go through that door we shall see things as they really are. Face to face.

> **What we see now is like a dim image in a mirror; then we shall see face to face. What I know now is only partial; then it will be complete—as complete as God's knowledge of me.**
>
> *1 Corinthians 13:12*

Now someone might say, 'Well, if death is so good then why don't you do it now? Take your own life?' But I don't believe that it's for me to decide when I die. God decides. And when the time comes it will be the right time for me to die.

I believe that on this side of the door God wants me to influence other people. To touch other people and to make their life a better life because of my being here.

But once I have fulfilled whatever it is that God has for me in store then I go through that door and I meet my Maker. When that happens I have the assurance and I have the faith to know that I will not tremble before my Father in heaven.

I revere my heavenly Father, and I hold him up on a pedestal. But I know when I go through that door that I shall not need to tremble. He will open his arms wide like the father of the prodigal son.

He will say, 'Welcome, my son! You have been in a far country, and you have done things that you shouldn't have done. You have had to walk by faith and not by sight. But now you see me face to face. You see me as I am.'

My Father's going to be there. My brother, Jesus, is going to be there. My brothers and sisters in the Lord are going to be there. All those I love are going to be there. And we are finally going to do what we were made for—to worship God.

'Worship God!' people say. 'What do you mean that you are going to worship God? What will you be doing?' And I don't know what we shall be doing or how we are all going to do it. But I know it's going to be a glorious time. I look forward so much to that time when I'm going to see him. I think I'm going to look back at my life and see the wrong turns that I've made. Jesus is going to show me. And I'll see the times when I was too scared to hold his hand and trust him.

My two little girls get so scared at times when we're doing things together. 'Come on,' I'll say to them. 'Don't be scared! I'm not going to let you fall. I'm going to be with you.' But sometimes they just won't trust me. So I pick them up and I do it with them—and then they see how they can do it.

I believe God will say to me, 'Kriss, I would have held your hand when you didn't see how it was going to work!' And I will say, 'Lord, I'm sorry. I just didn't believe . . .'

One day we shall all stand in front of the great white throne of judgment. We shall meet God there and give an account of our life. 'Everyone must die once, and after that be judged by God,' the Bible says (Hebrews 9:27).

The one who is going to be our judge is Jesus. No one will ever be able to say to Jesus, 'You don't know what it's like down there.' Because he does know. That's one of the reasons why God had to become a man. Jesus had to be able to empathize with you and with me. Otherwise man could say to God, 'It's all right for you up in heaven—but down there it was hell on earth.' Now God can say, 'I've been there—and none of you guys have been through what I've been through.'

Jesus Christ died for us—so that we could have life. On the cross God was in Christ reconciling the world to himself, and making friends out of the people who were his enemies.

When someone becomes a Christian he becomes a brand new person inside. He is not the same any more. A new life has begun!

All these new things are from God, who brought us back to himself through what Christ Jesus did. And God has given us the privilege of urging everyone to come into his favour and be reconciled to him. For God was in Christ, restoring the world to himself, no longer

counting men's sins against them but blotting them out. This is the wonderful message he has given us to tell others. We are Christ's ambassadors. God is using us to speak to you: we beg you, as though Christ himself were here pleading with you, receive the love he offers you—be reconciled to God. For God took the sinless Christ and poured into him our sins. Then, in exchange, he poured God's goodness into us!

2 Corinthians 5:17–21 (Living Bible)

We all have different sorts of experiences. But one experience is common to all of us. Death is the destiny of every man and of every woman. People think this life is going to go on for ever and ever. One more doughnut! One more go in the slot machine! Then one day 'Boom!' Death is at the door and they are not prepared.

They have got the wrong clothes on. They never got ready for the race. They weren't on their starting blocks and they were in the wrong lane. They took drugs. They did the things that disqualified them from life.

We have got to have the right clothes on—and God will give them to us. 'My soul rejoices in my God. For he has clothed me with garments of salvation and arrayed me in a robe of righteousness' (Isaiah 61:10, NIV).

We have got to get in the right lane, and to run the race, and to cross the line. St Paul did it—and if we get on the right track we can do it too. It's a great race— and Jesus is a great God!

As for me, my life is already being poured out on the altar, and the hour for my departure is upon me. I have run the great race, I have finished the course, I have kept the faith. And now there awaits me the garland of righteousness which the Lord, the righteous Judge, will award to me on the great day, and not to me alone, but to all who have set ther hearts on his coming appearance.

2 Timothy 4:6–8 (REB)

Epilogue:

Getting on track with the Christian life

If you want to become a Christian, then turn back to page 19 at the end of 'On track with Jesus'. I've said there how you can ask Jesus to come into your life—and if you do that you will find that everything else gets into the right perspective. It's not that all your problems will disappear—but you'll have someone with you to help you to cope with them.

Once you have started your new life as a Christian there are three very important things that you need to know—three things that the young Christian needs to do.

1. Have fellowship

First of all, tune in with like-minded people—with other Christians. Then meet on a regular basis—ideally once a week—and read the Bible, pray, and talk through the issues that you are experiencing in your life.

Getting together with other Christians is commonly called Church! But I'm not just talking about going to church on Sunday, important though that is—because church is one of the places where we worship God and are given teaching from trained ministers. I'm talking about fellowship—and it is important to understand that the Church isn't the building, or the rituals that go along with an established institution. The Church is people—and Christian fellowship is about communication with those people.

When two or three Christians can get together on a regular basis then they're a church. If one of them is more experienced than the others, or in the ministry, then that's fine. But that isn't always possible.

Fellowship really means 'sharing in the same things'. Like several people sharing the same dish in a Chinese meal, Christians are sharing the same life—the life of Jesus. So one of the things that is very important is regular meeting with other Christians, and having a relationship with one another. Talk through what you heard when you were in church—and talk to one another about what God has done for you this week. You'll find that it's uplifting and upbuilding. And it's not instead of church on Sunday—but in conjunction with going to church.

Then there are two more important things, because our relationship with God develops through prayer and through Bible reading.

2. Pray

This weekend I met a guy I hadn't seen for twenty-five years. He was an 'uncle' in the children's home that I lived in (where they called the home leaders uncles and aunties). He is a Franciscan monk now, Brother Simon Christopher, and I met him at an evangelistic crusade.

He was doing a seminar on prayer, and afterwards I sat with him and told him that for me prayer is talking to God just like I was talking to him, and that I'm always speaking to God but I don't have a very deep prayer life. I can't pray for an hour at a stretch like some people do.

He said to me, 'Kriss, over the past twenty-five years I have found that the power of prayer is in being able to listen. It's what you hear and not just in what you say. If you can hear what God says, and then do what he says, then the power of prayer is shown. Getting used to prayer is getting used to sitting down—and being able to hear and being able to listen. It's not just a monologue but a dialogue.'

3. Read the Bible

The next thing is to spend time each day reading a small portion of scripture. It may only be a couple of verses—but it's very important to do it. Then think of what it would mean to the people it was written to. Ask yourself, 'What was this guy trying to say to the people it was written to?' Then ask, 'What is God saying to me through it. And how does that affect my life today.' Pray that you'll understand—and listen to what he says to you.

If you have enjoyed reading and using *Kriss Akabusi on Track With the Bible*, you may wish to know that BRF produce a regular series of Bible reading notes, *New Daylight*, which is published three times a year (in January, May and September) and contains printed Bible passages, brief comments and prayers. *New Daylight* is also available in a large print version.

Copies of *New Daylight* may be obtained from your local Christian bookshop or by subscription direct from BRF.

A **FREE SAMPLE COPY** of *New Daylight* containing two weeks of readings may be obtained by sending an A5 SAE marked 'New Daylight' to BRF.

For more information about *New Daylight* and the full range of BRF publications, write to: The Bible Reading Fellowship, Peter's Way, Sandy Lane West, OXFORD OX4 5HG (Tel: 01865 748227)